"Hey, little artist and color explorers! Welcome to 'Fantastic Friends Coloring,' where the magic of imagination meets the power of your crayons! A big shoutout to all the super-creative kiddos and their grown-up pals for joining us on this vibrant adventure. Get ready to sprinkle life into these pages with your colorful wizardry. Let your imagination run wild and let the coloring bonanza begin! Thank you for bringing your artistic awesomeness to our coloring party – let's make every page as fantastic as you are!"

Oli Pereira
2024

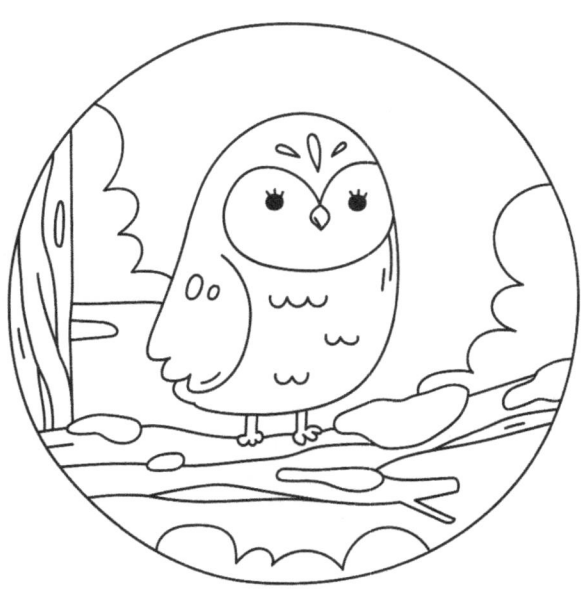
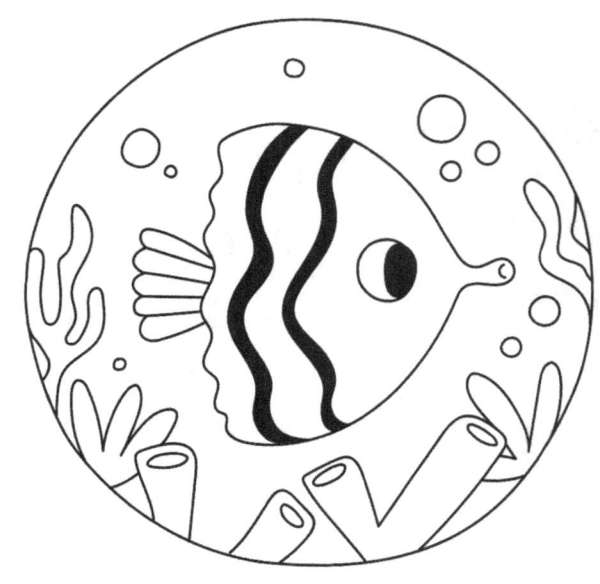

This Book Belongs to:

○————————————————————————————○

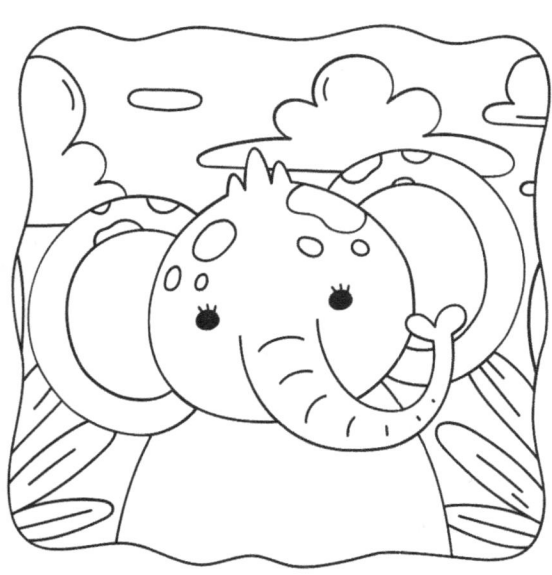
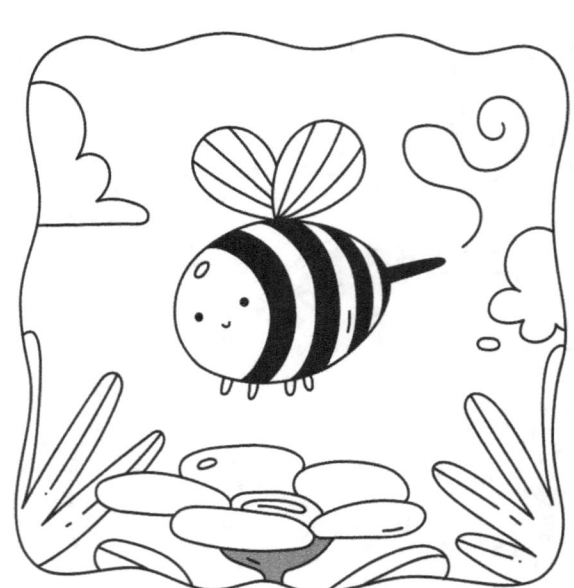

Test Color Page

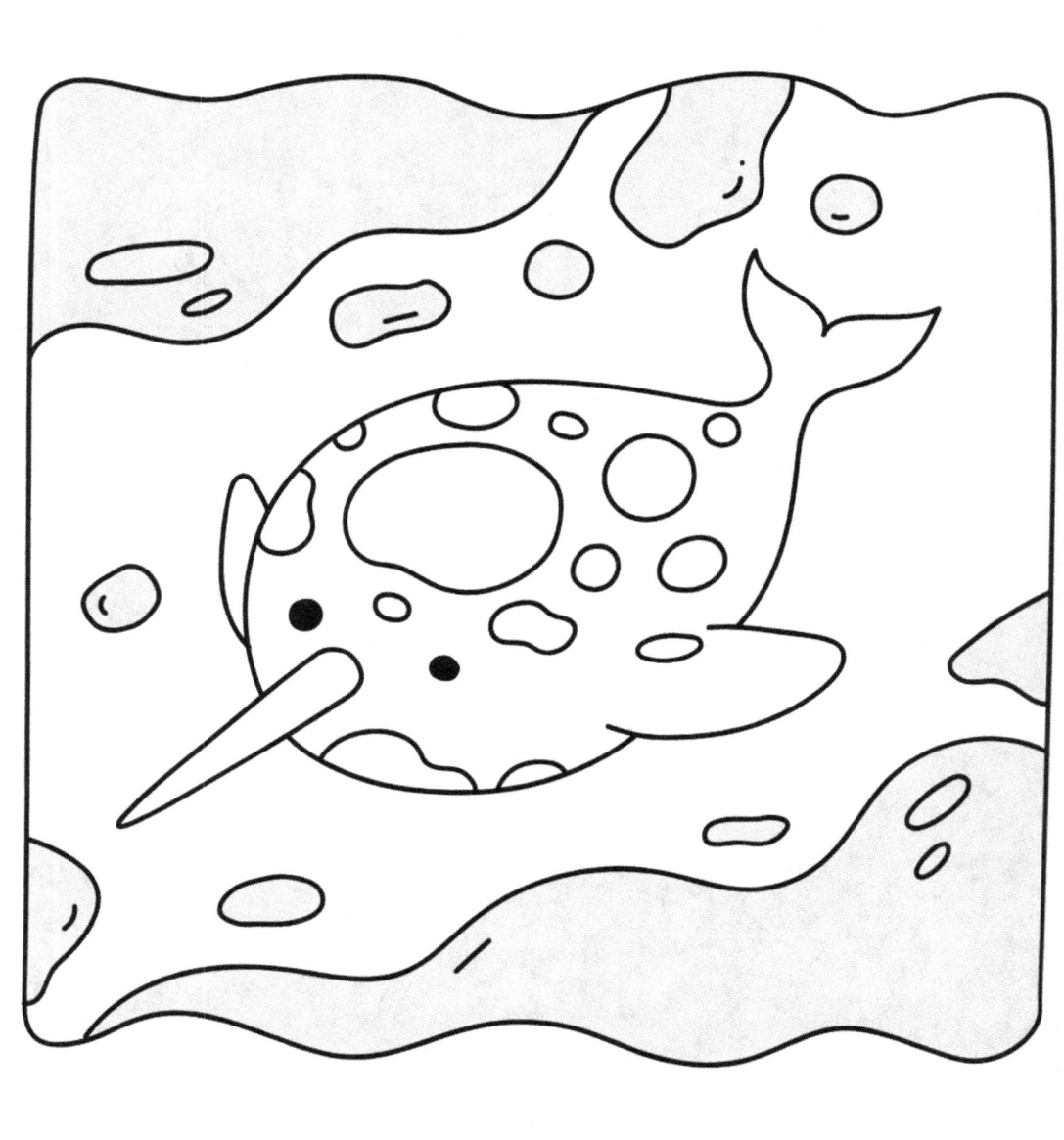

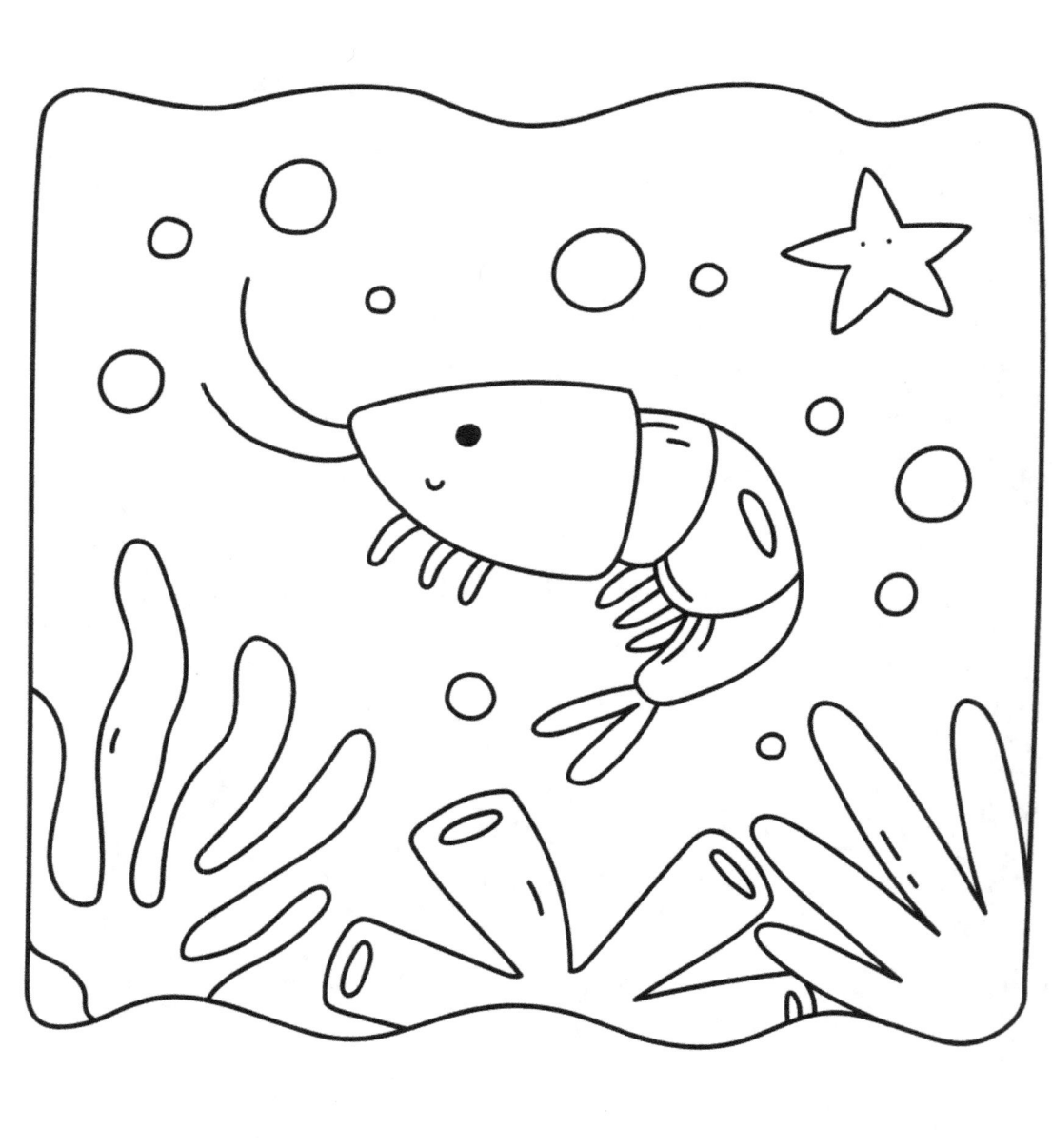

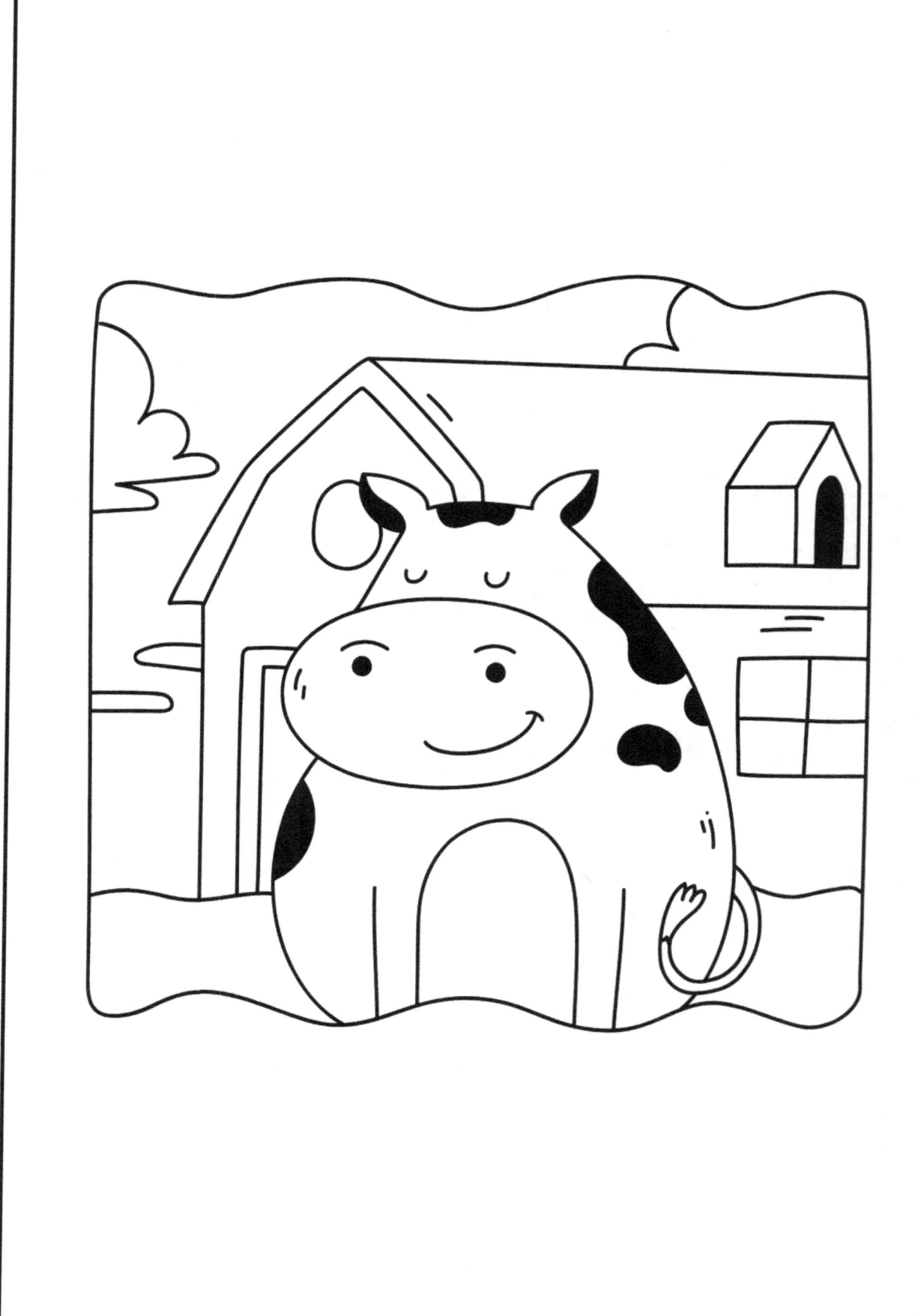

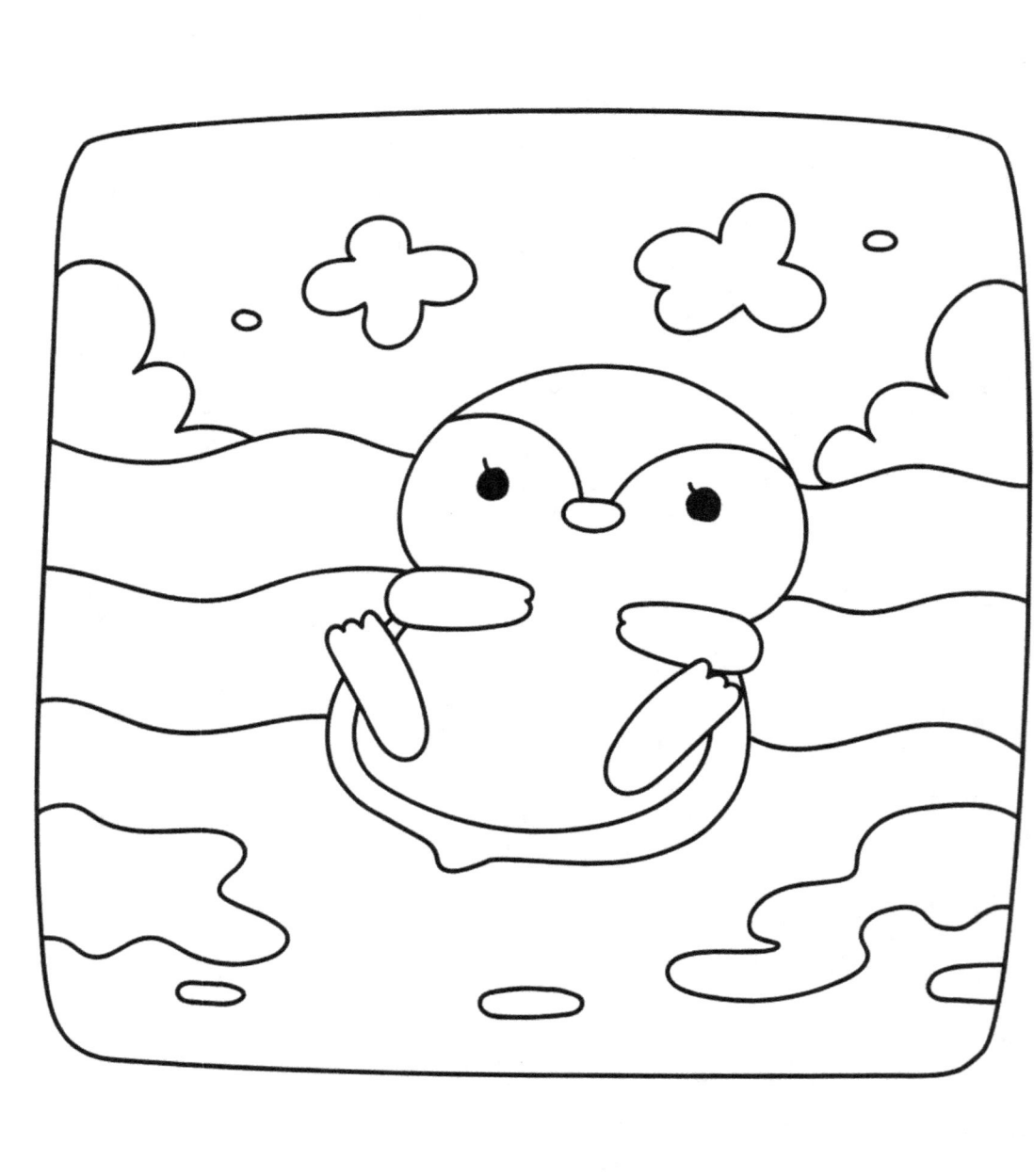

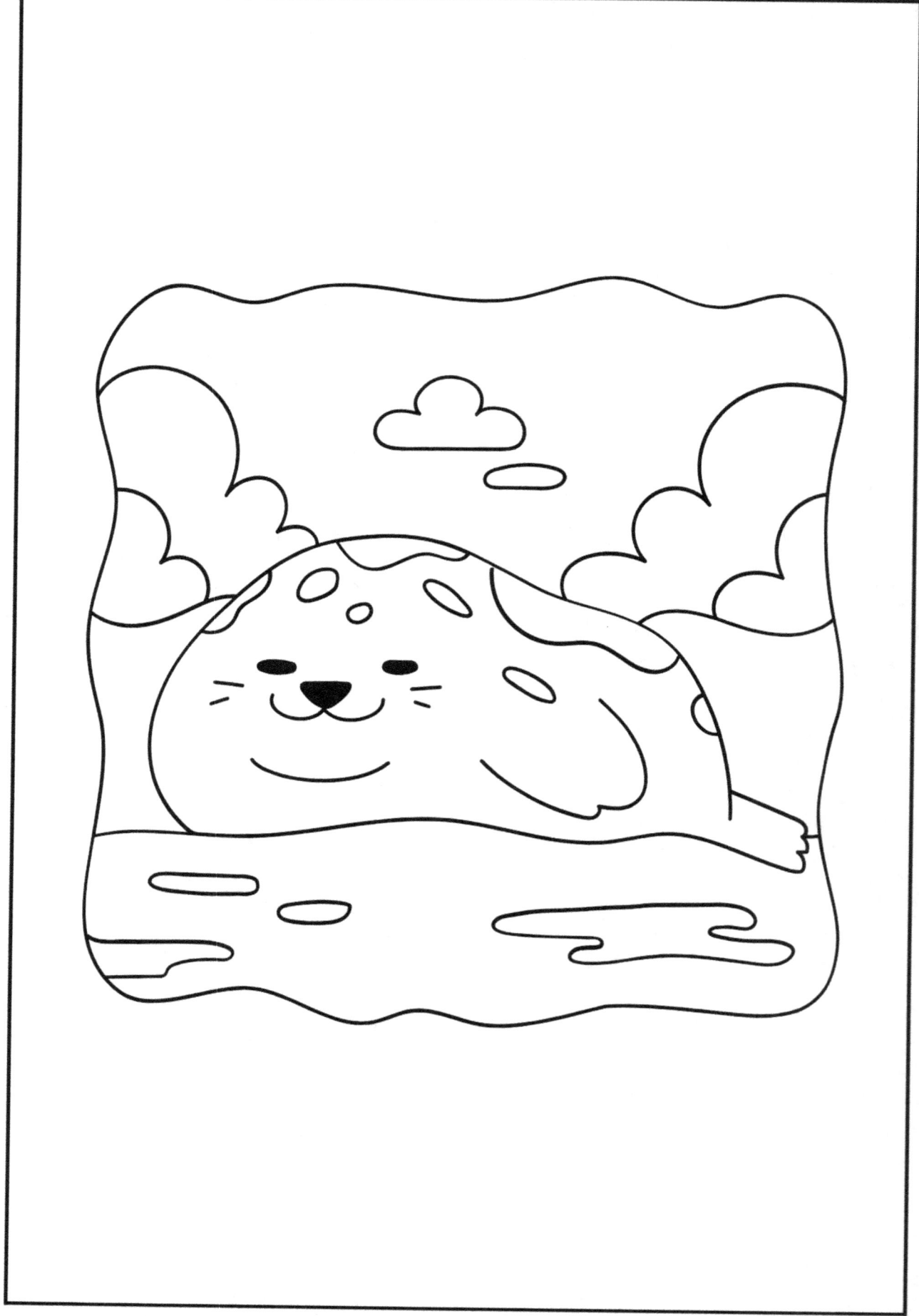

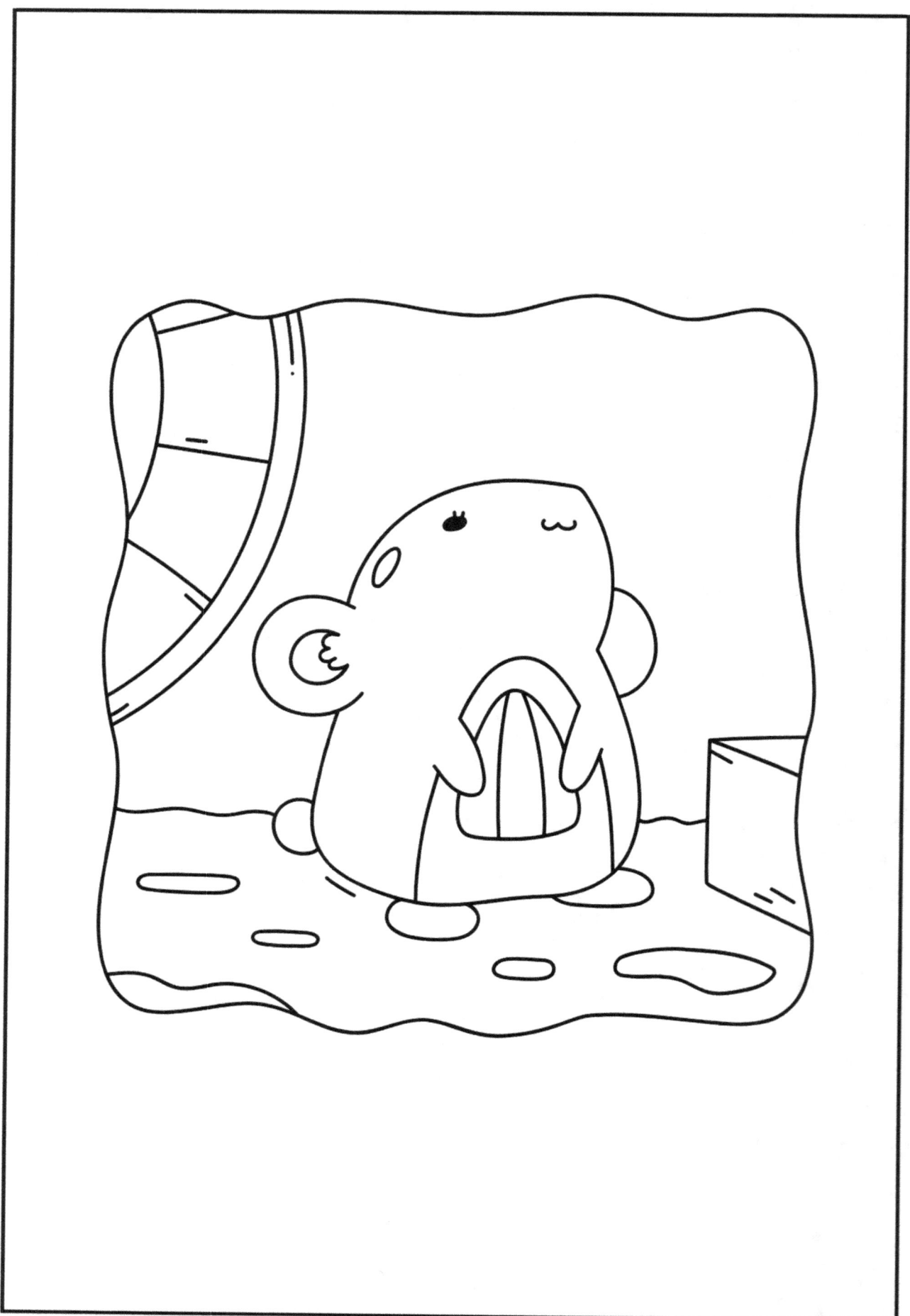

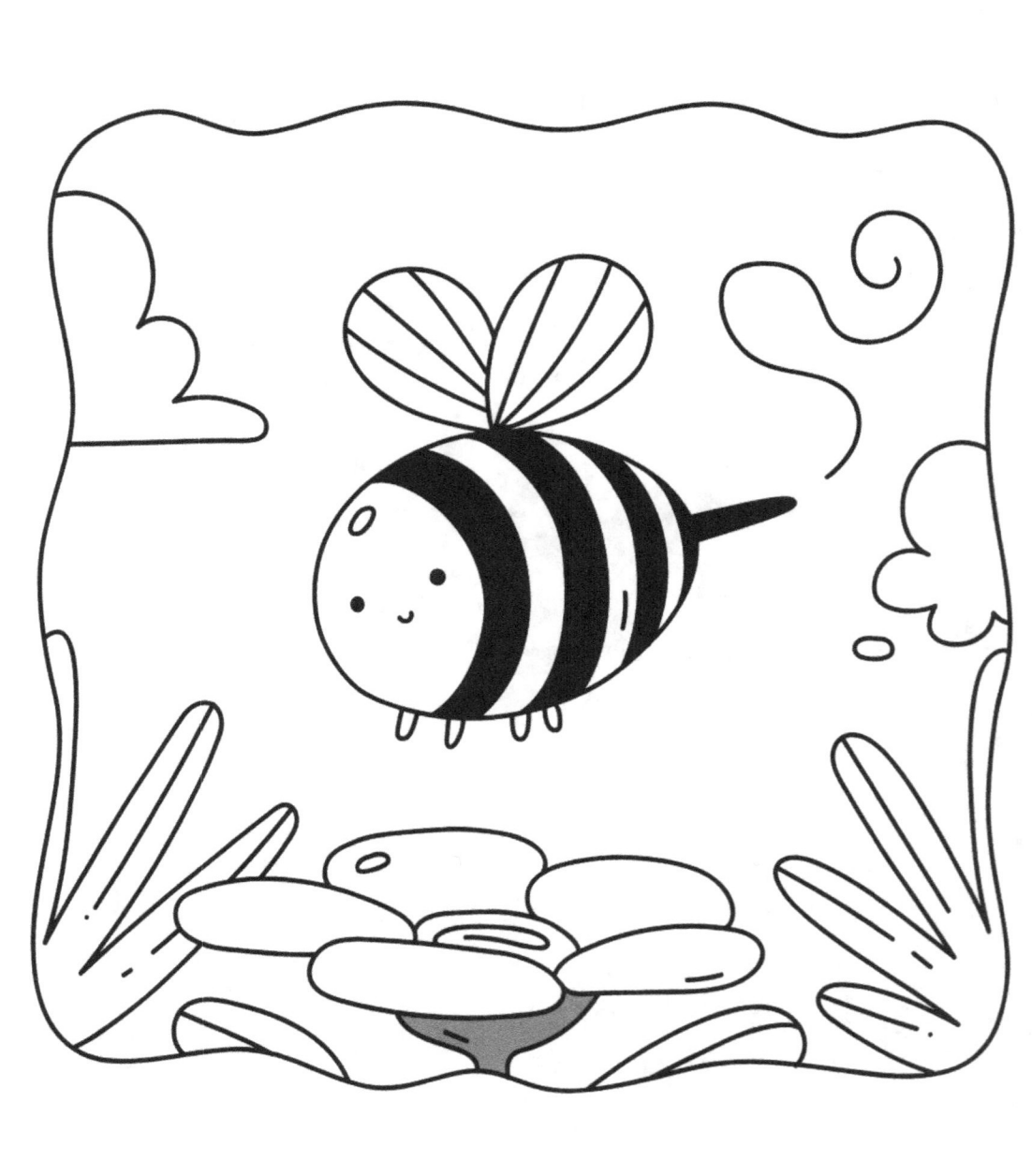

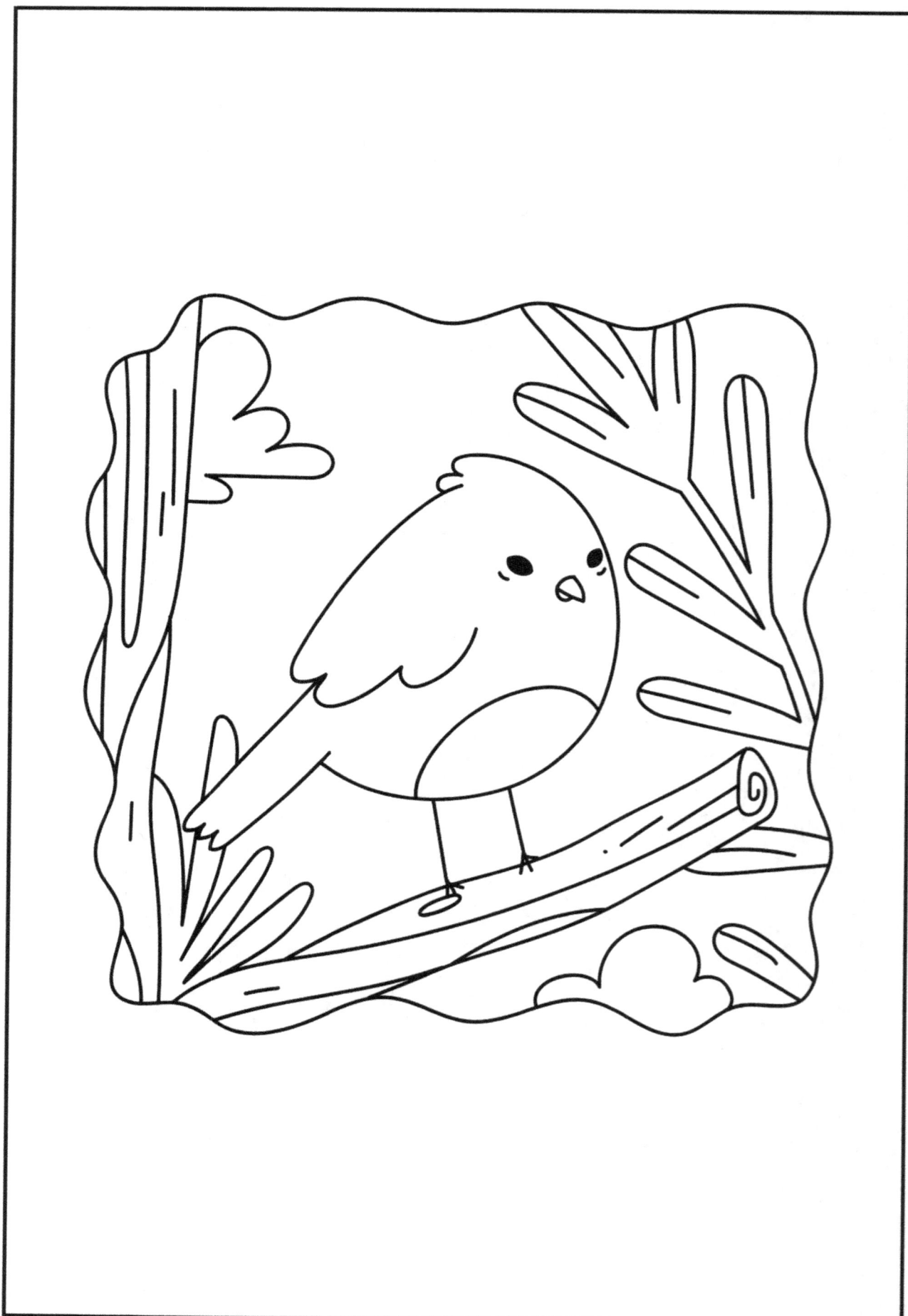

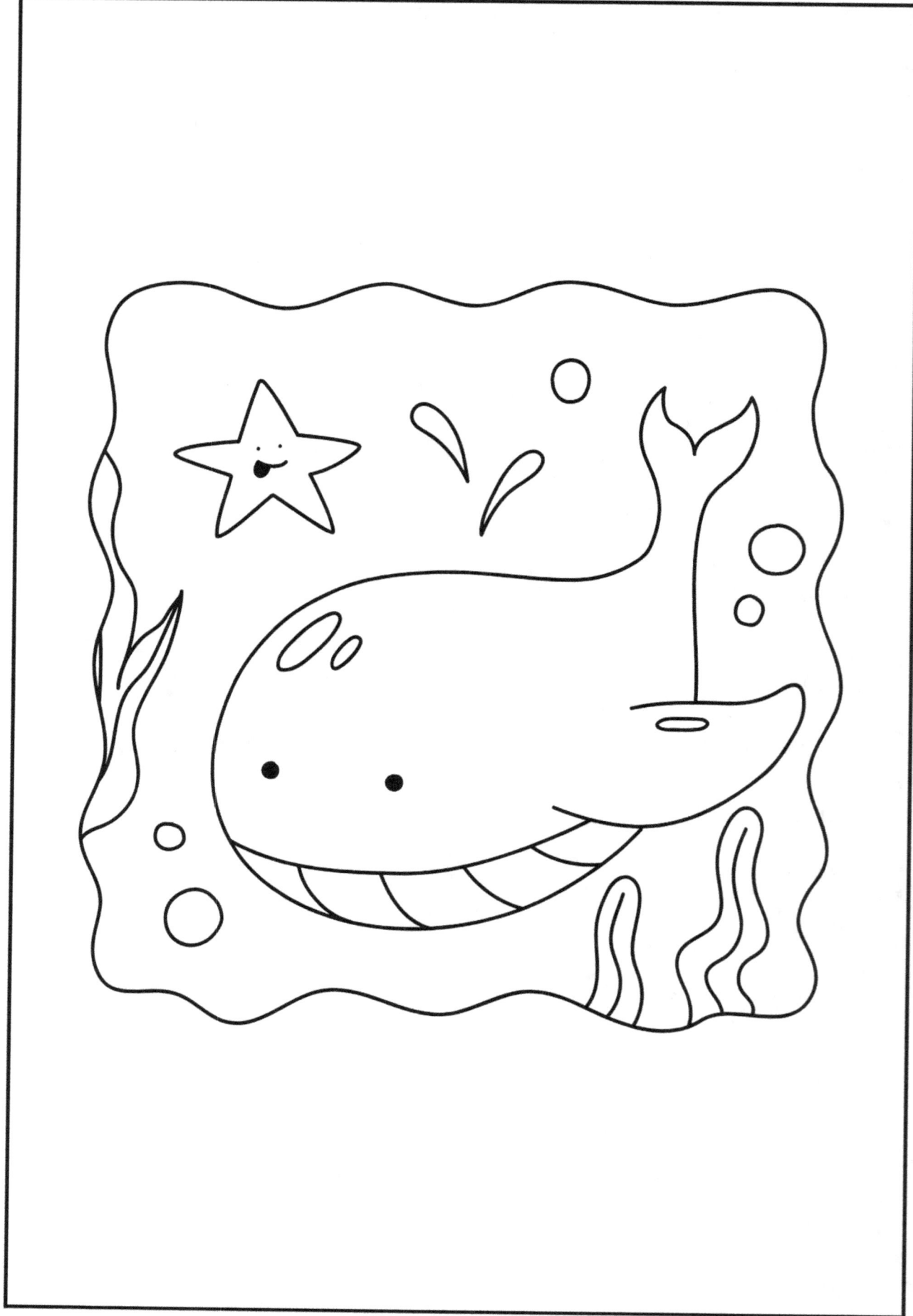

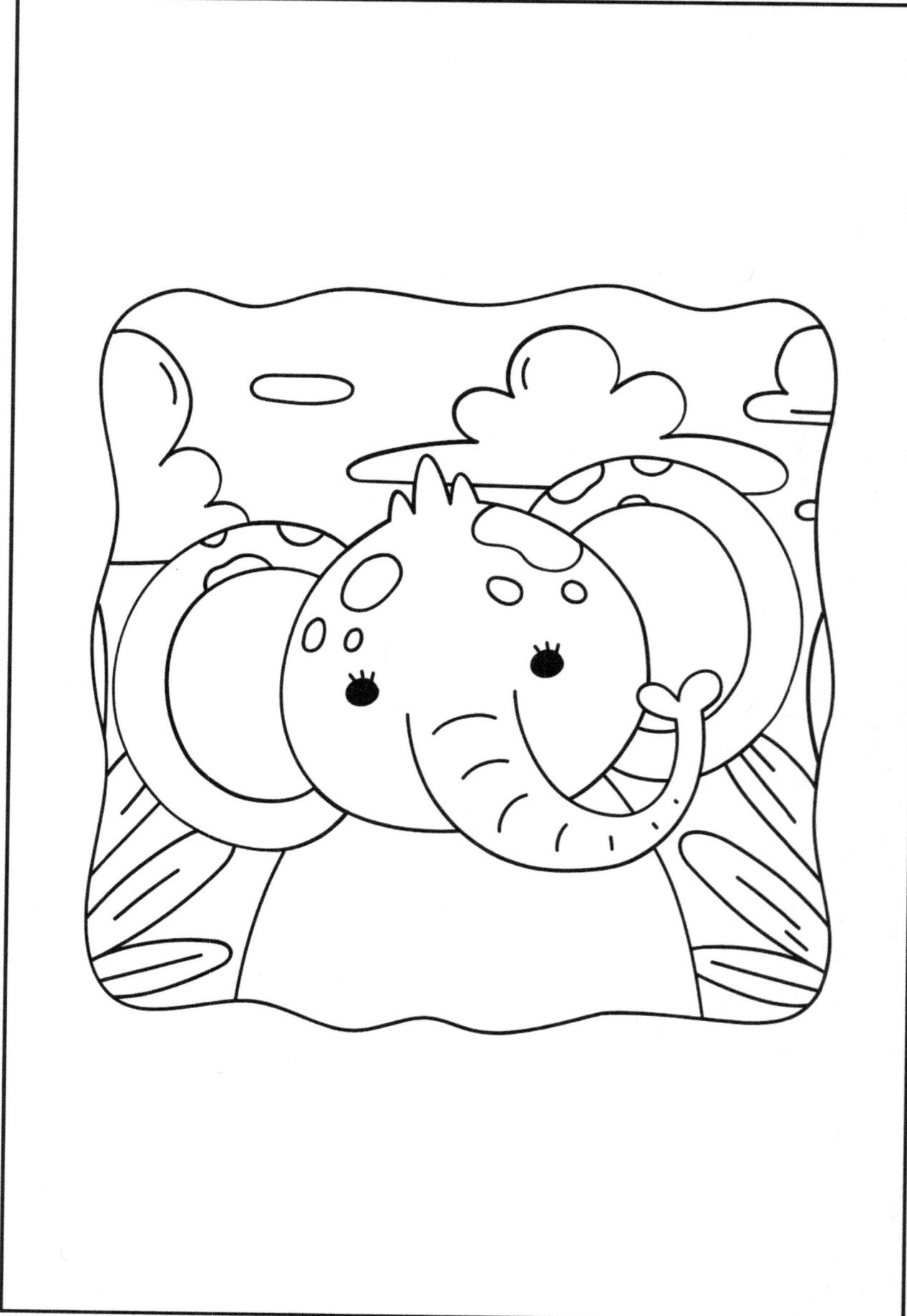

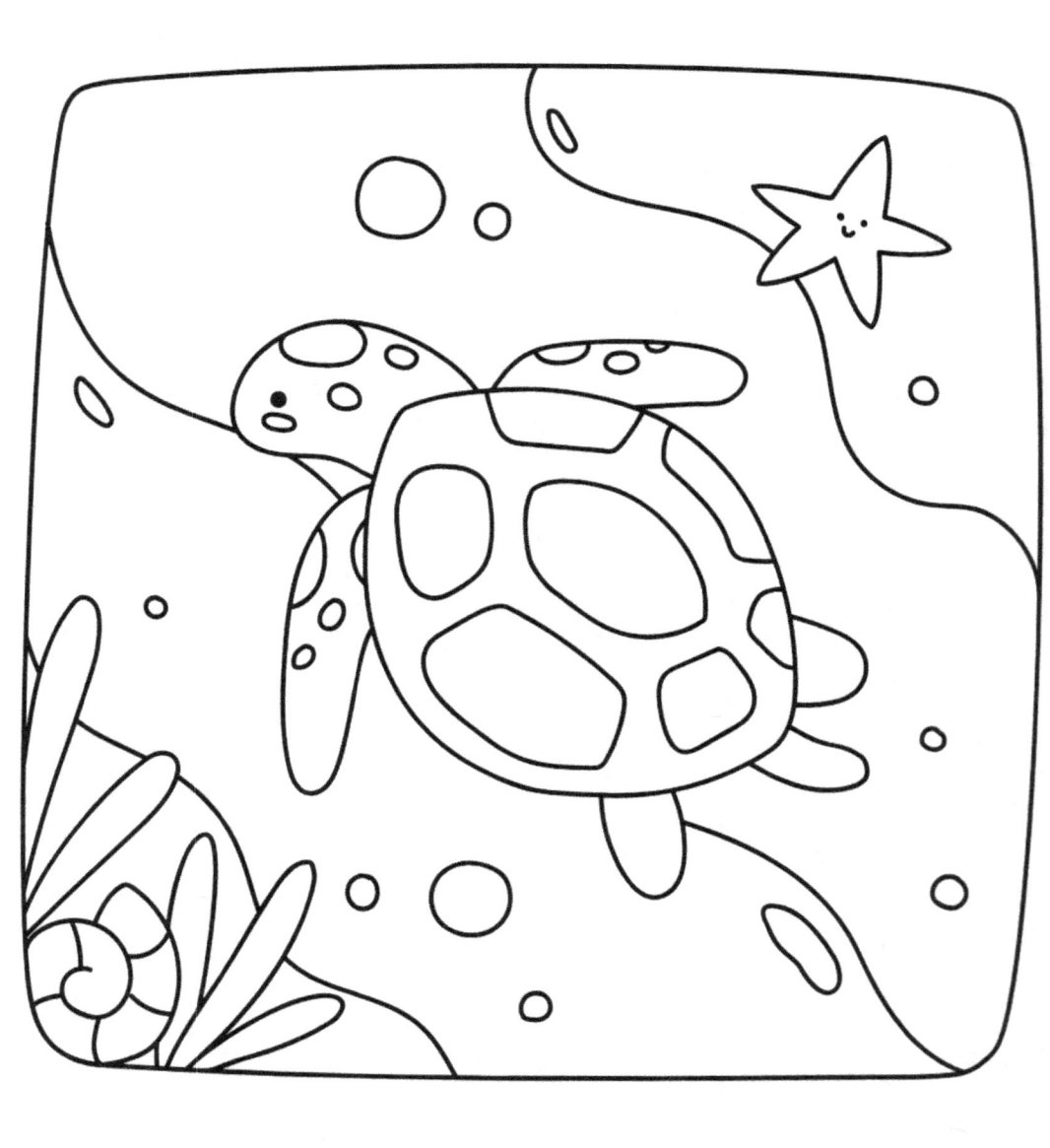

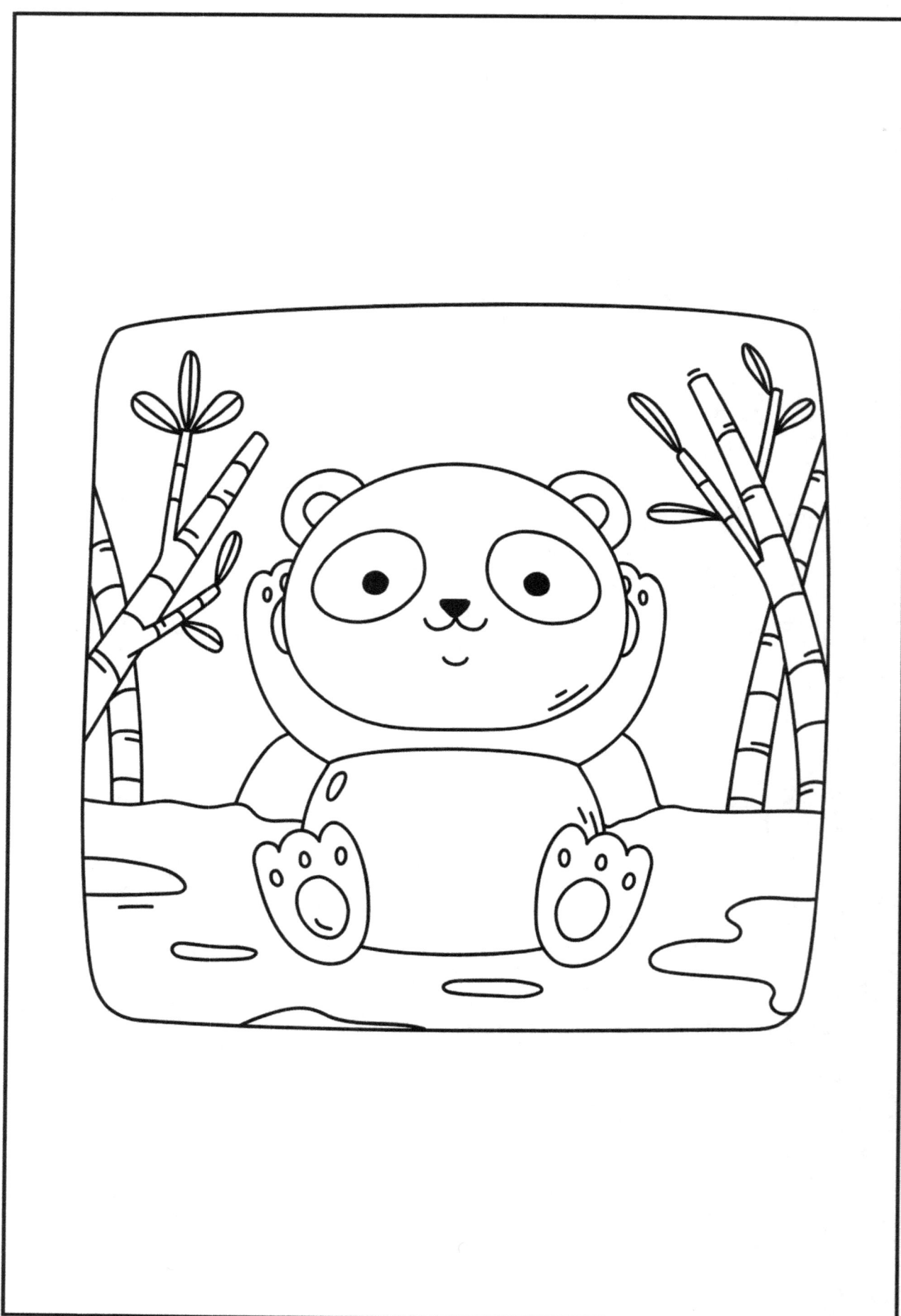

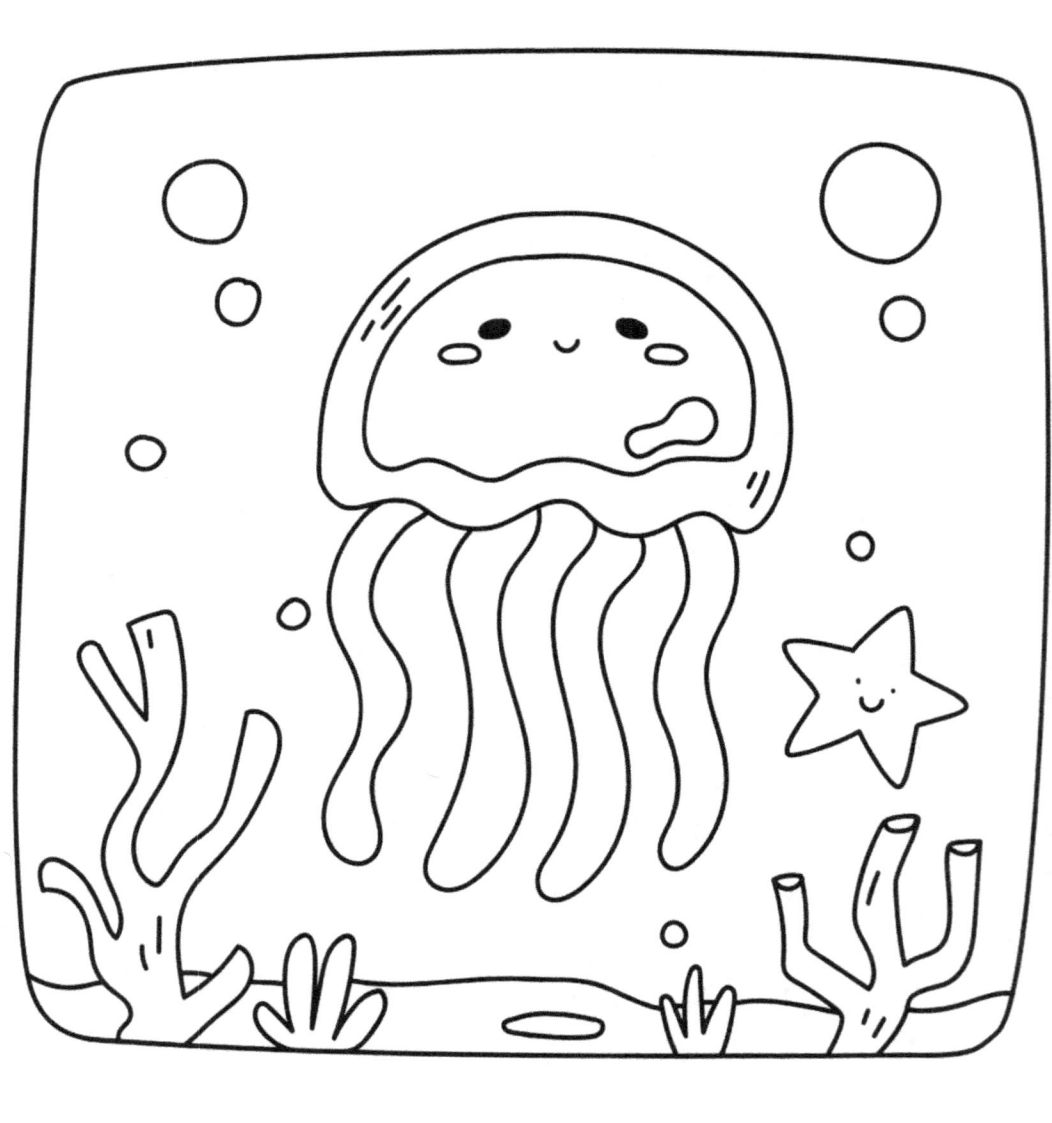

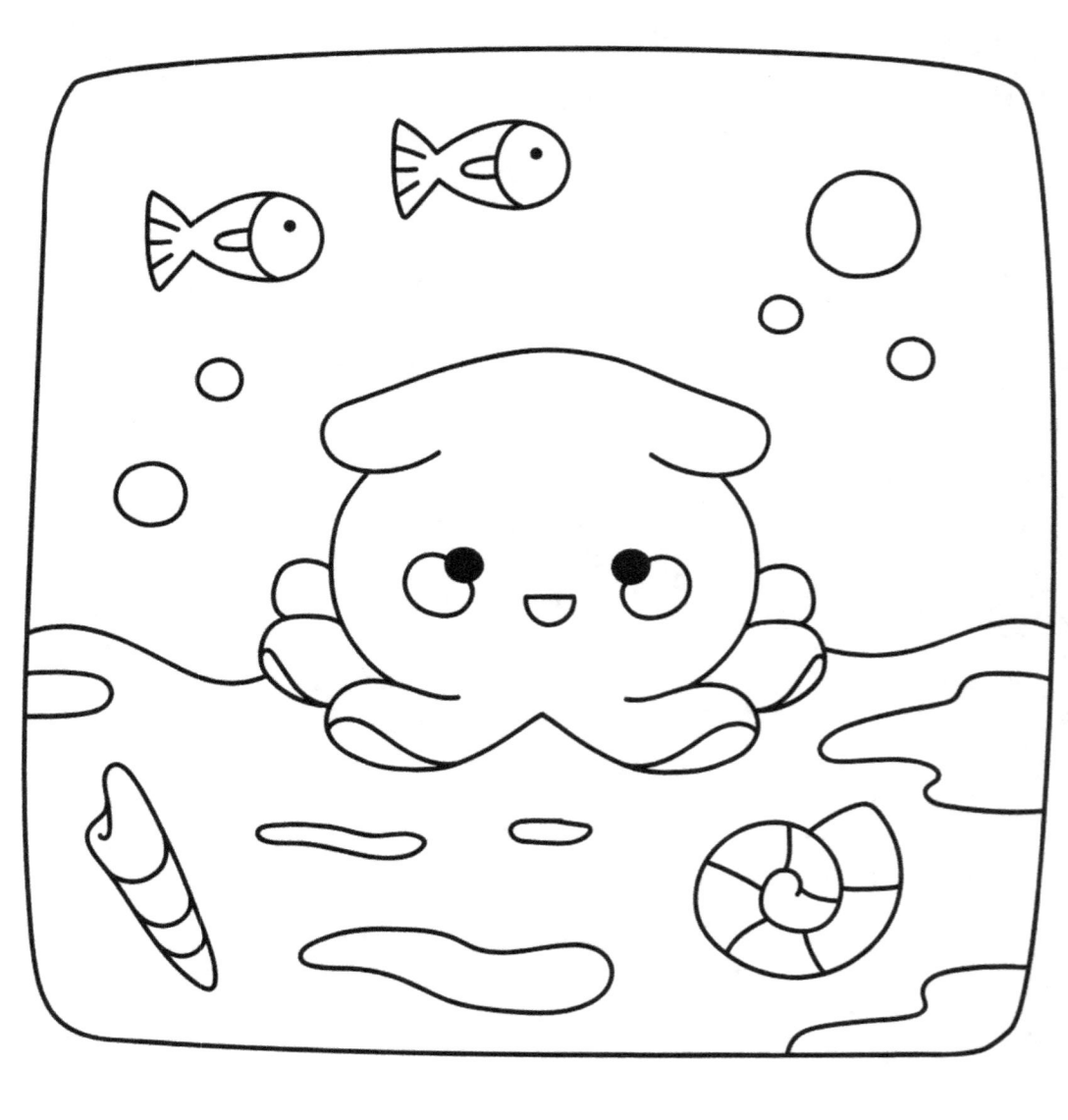

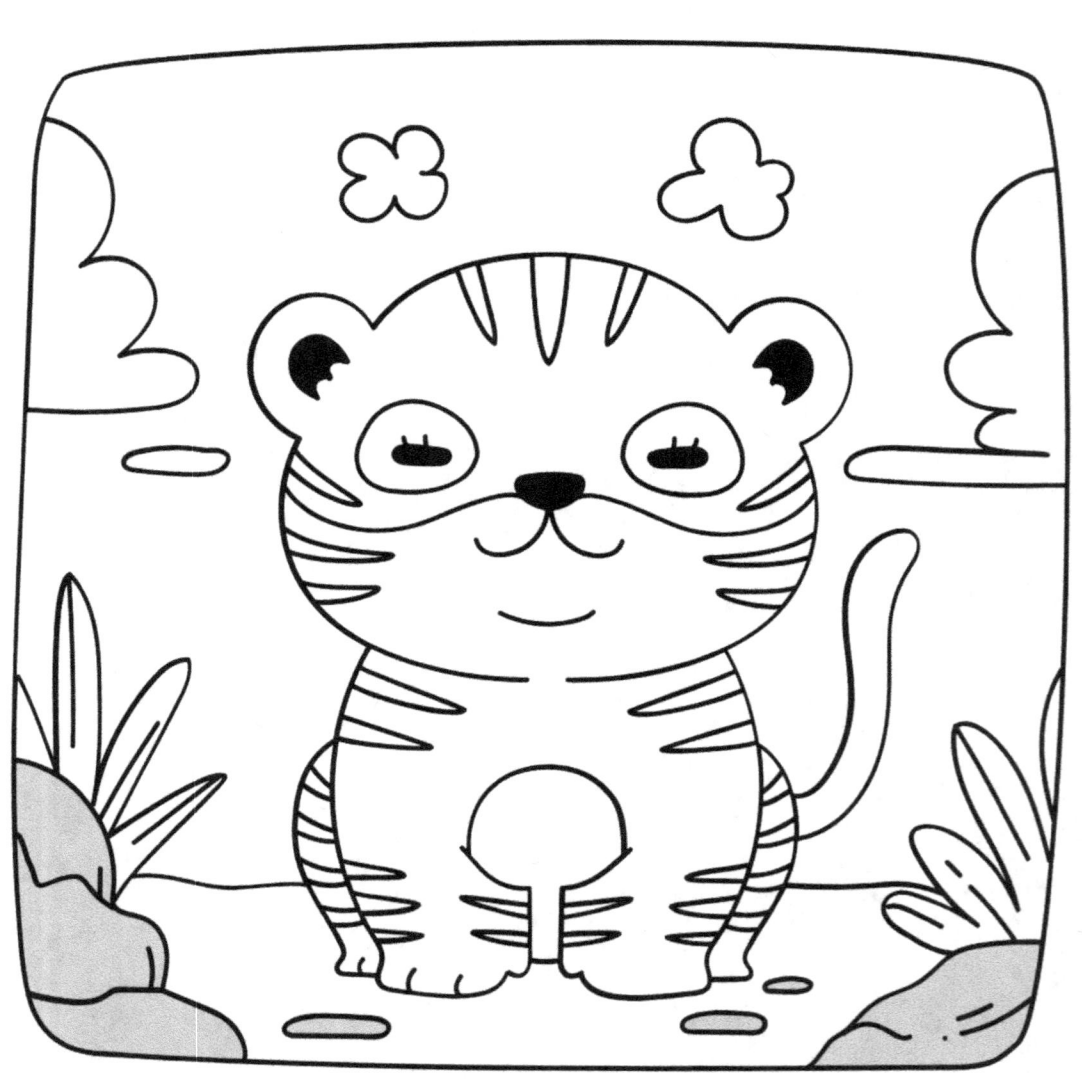

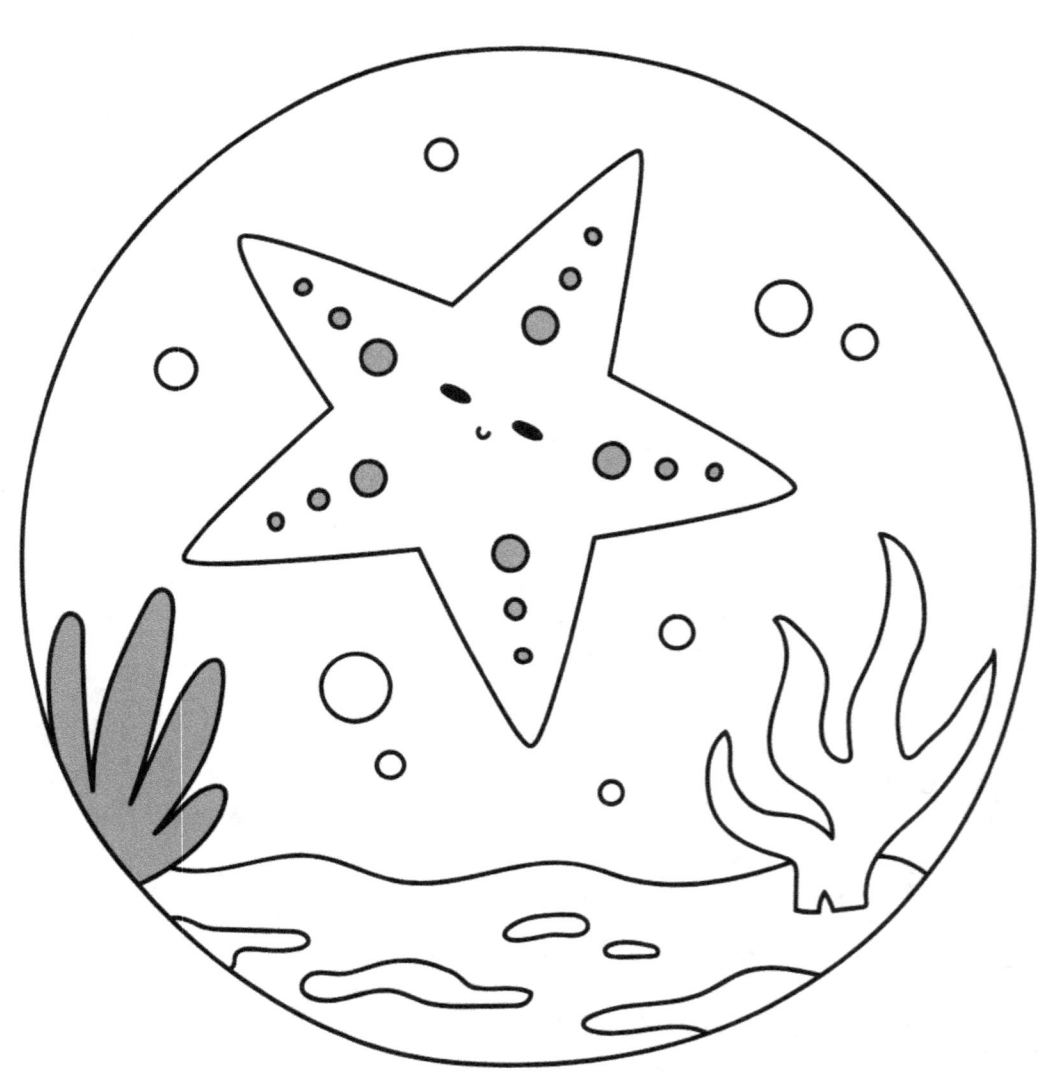

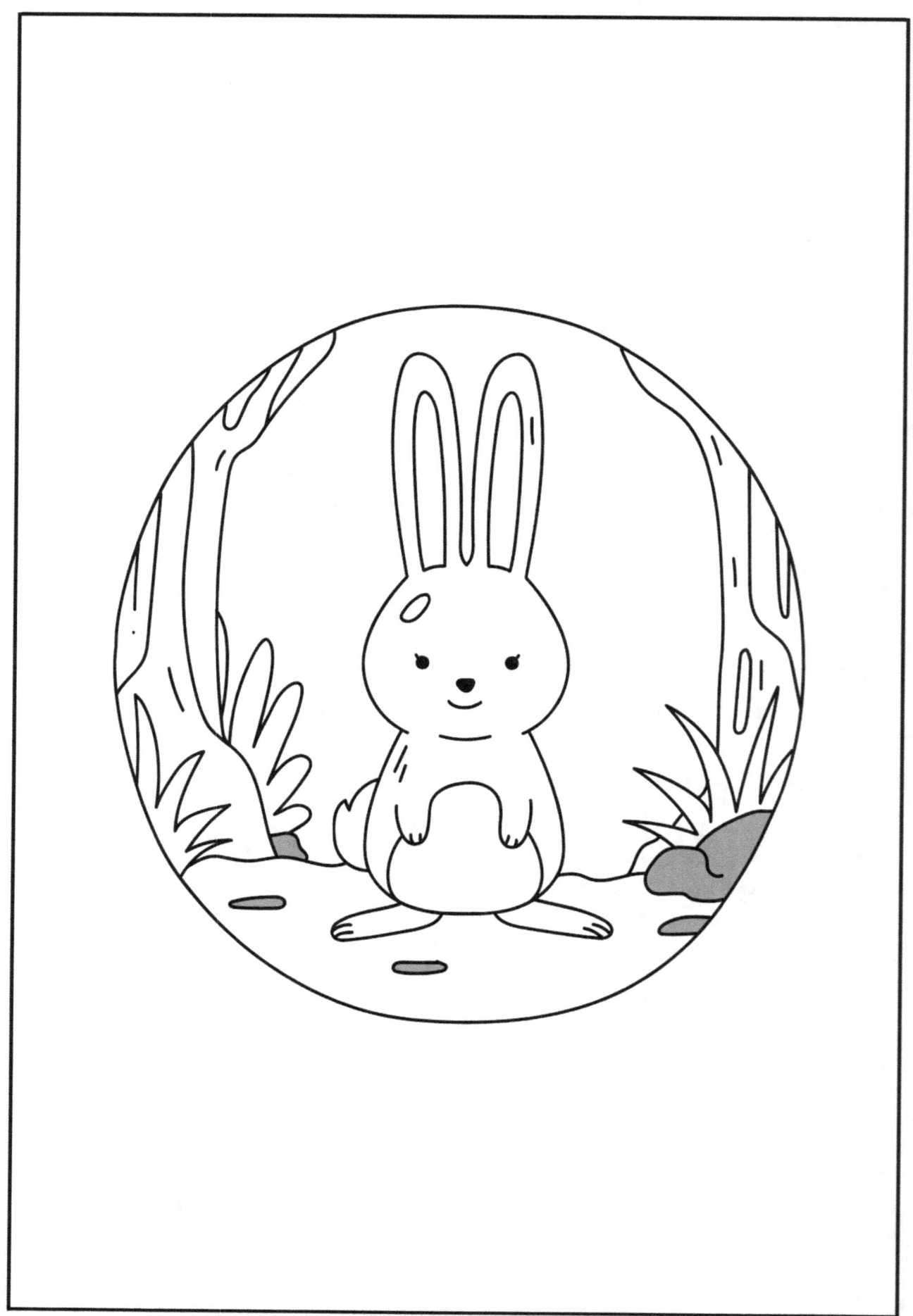

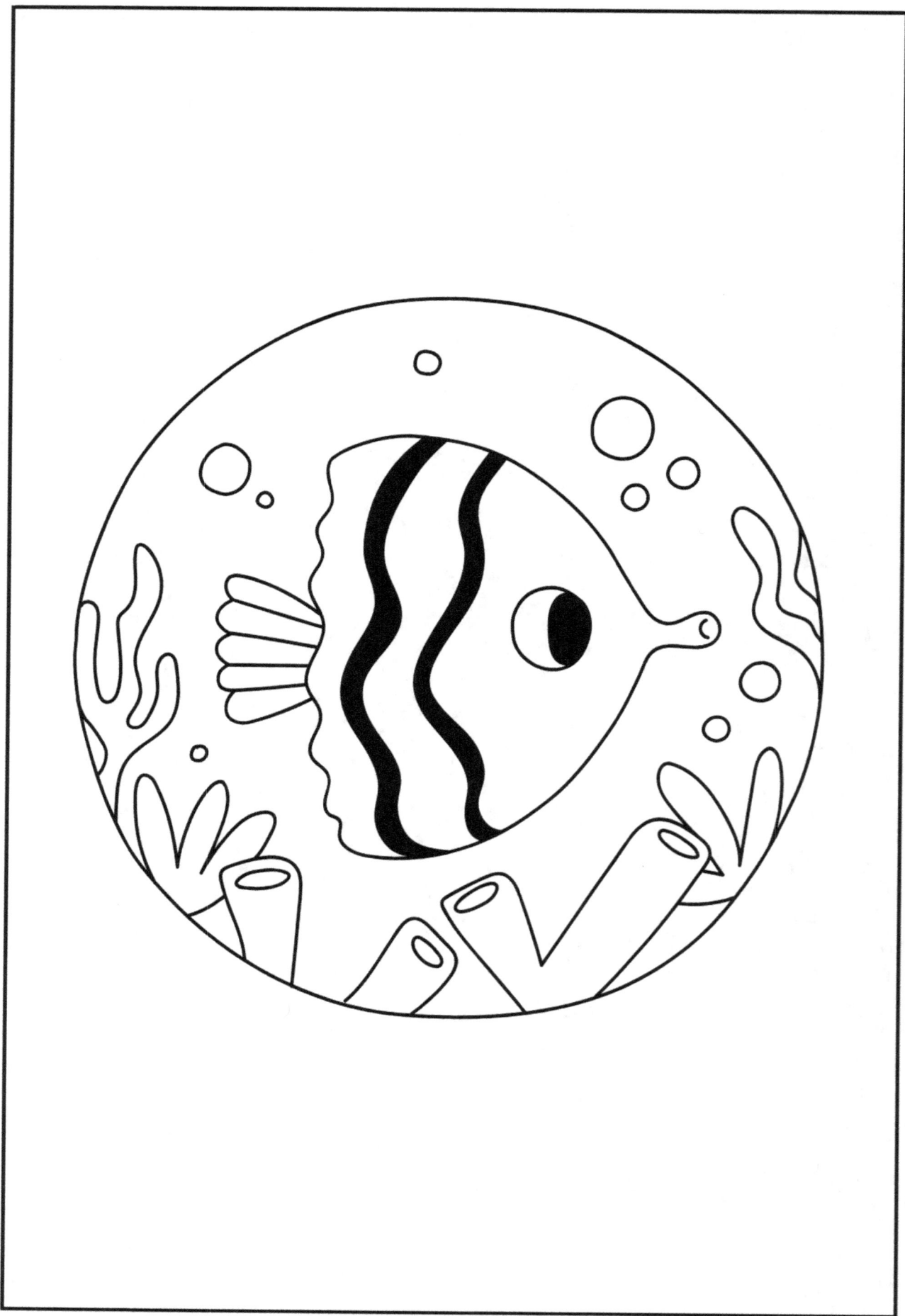

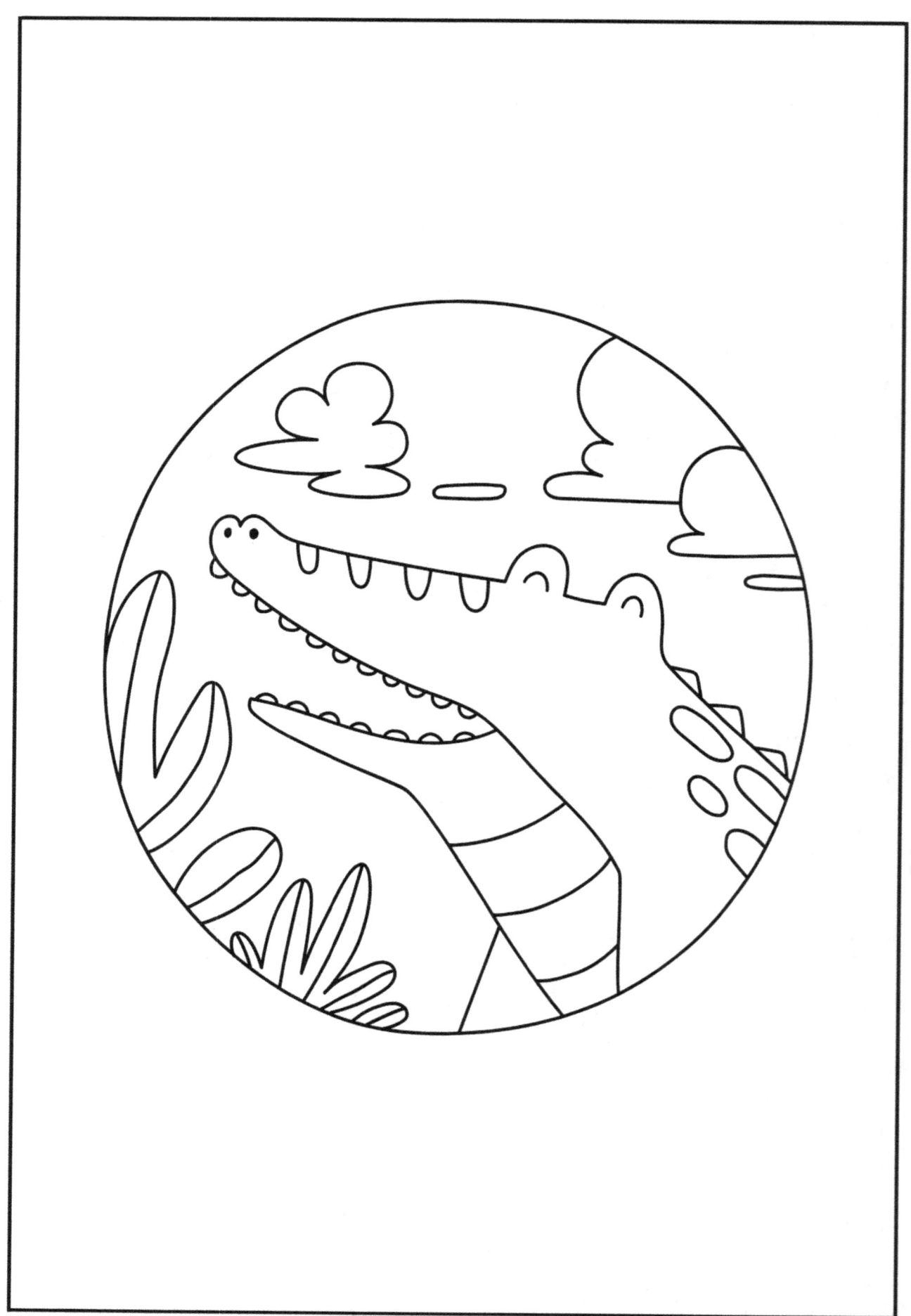

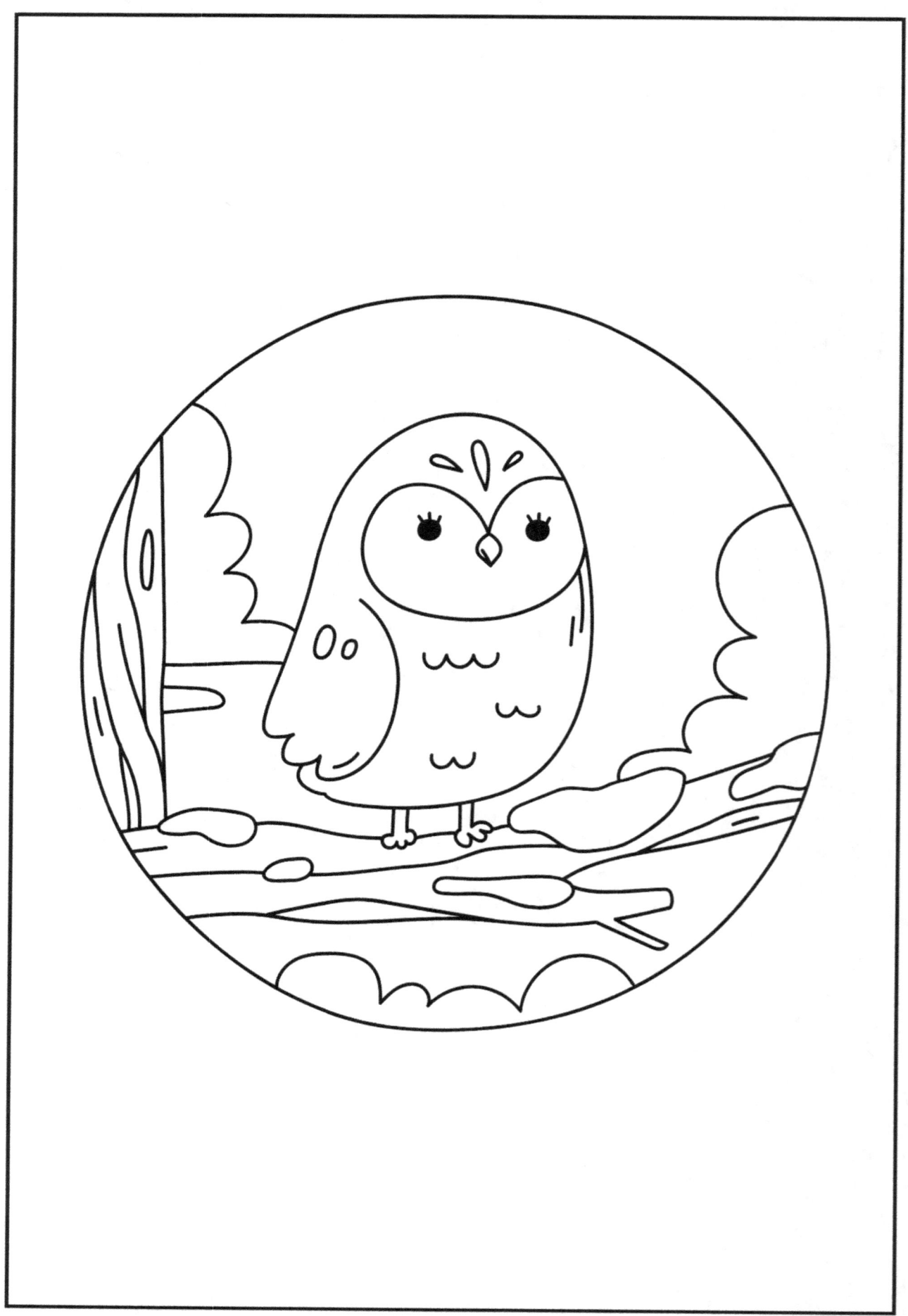

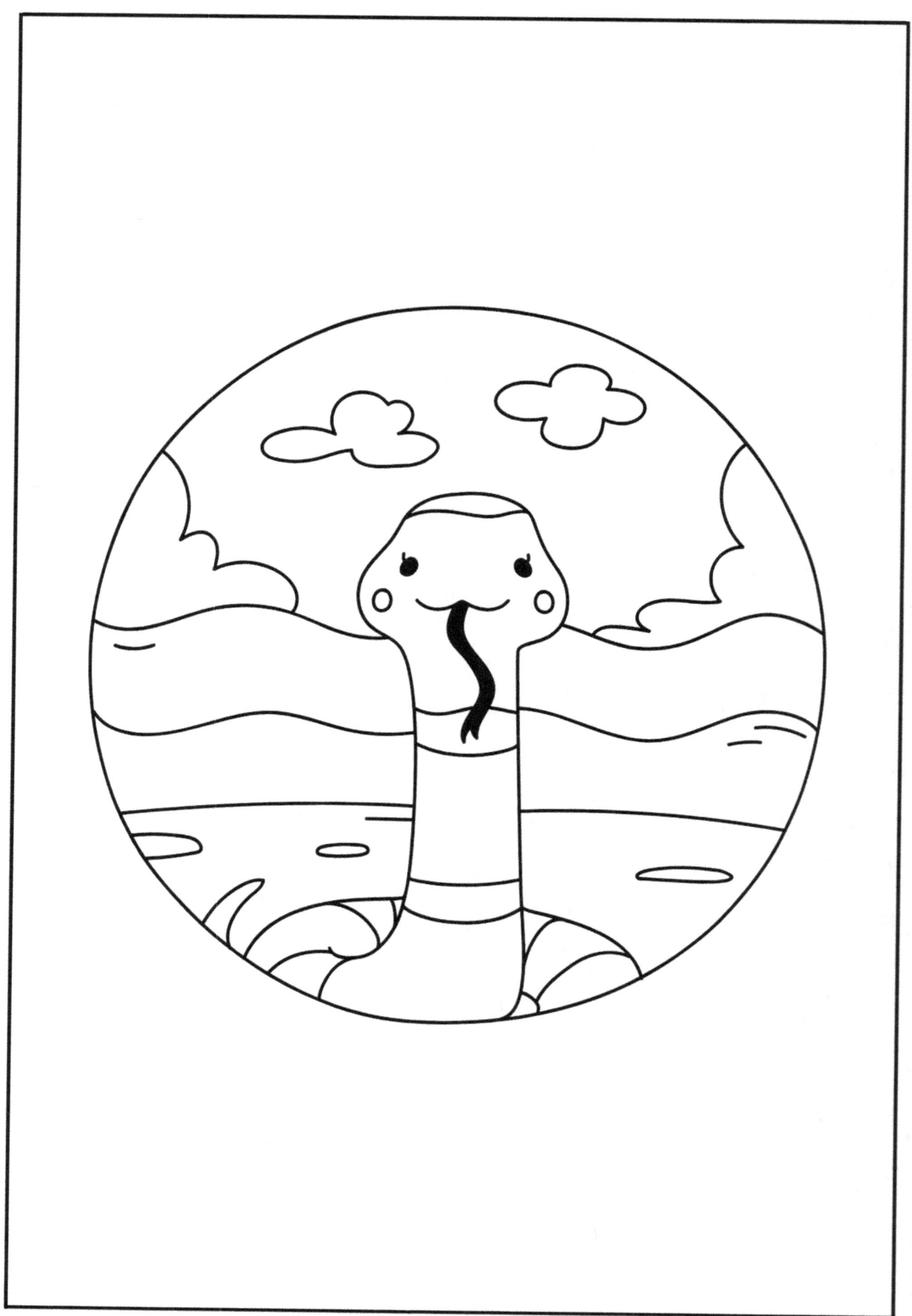

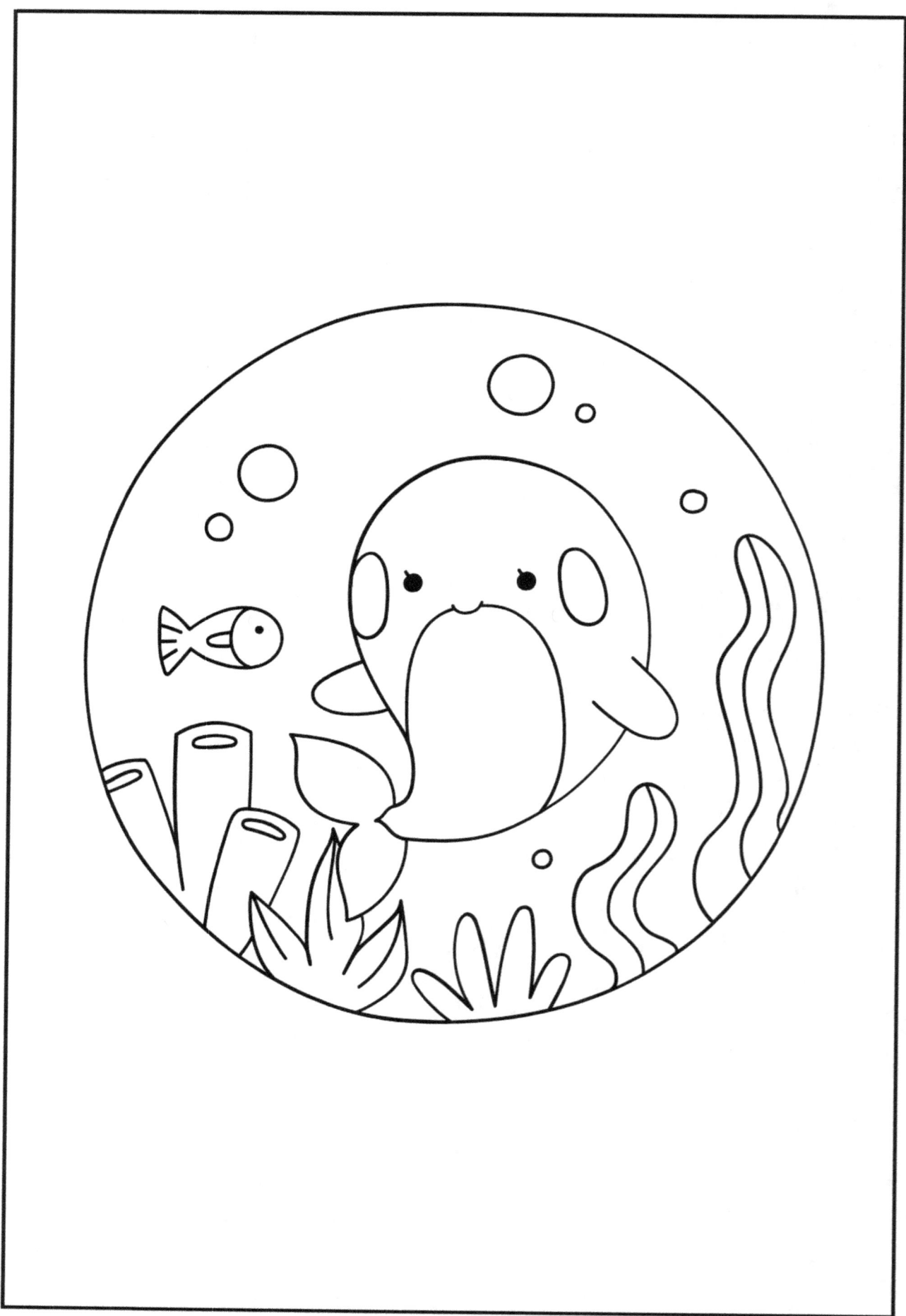

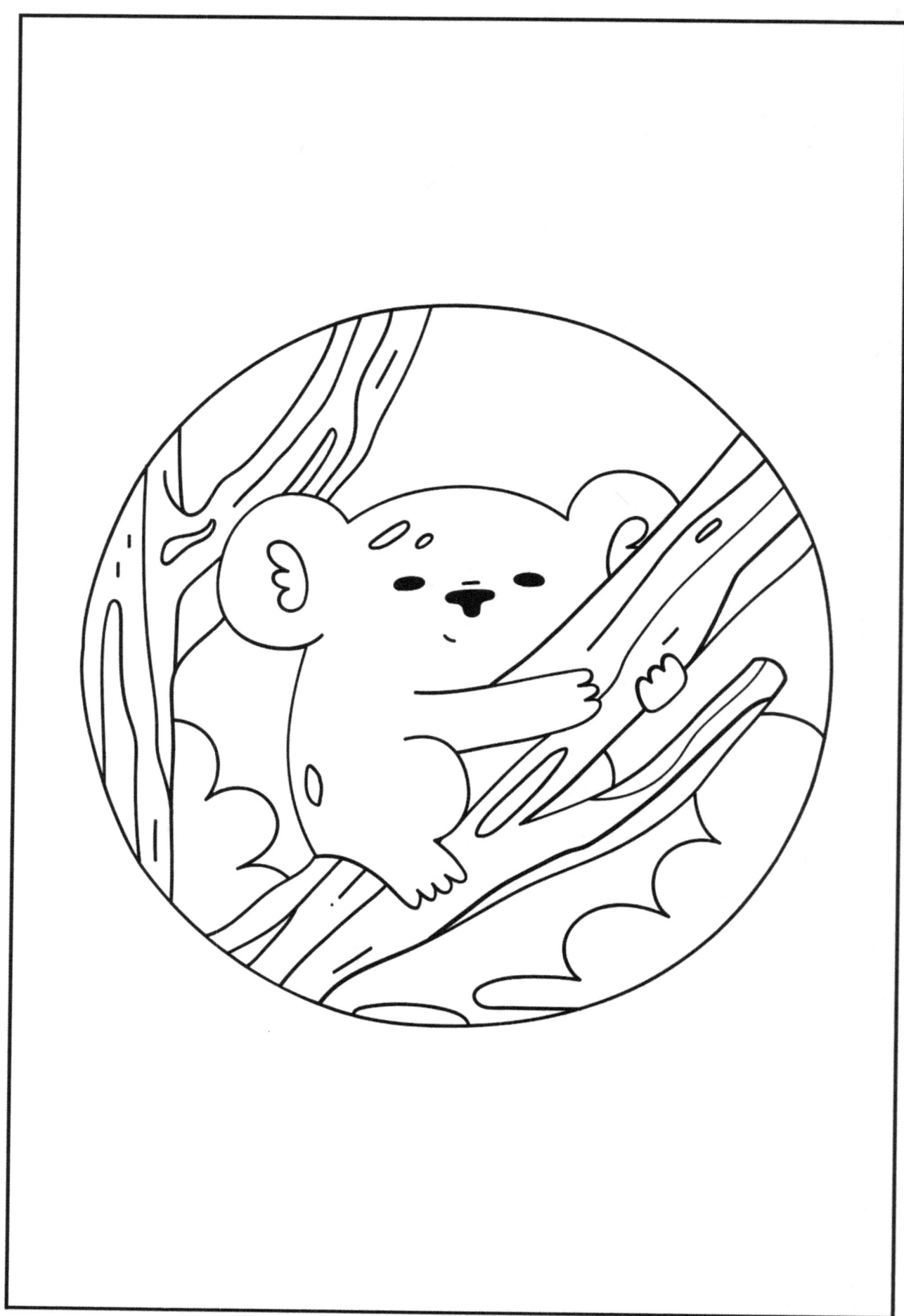

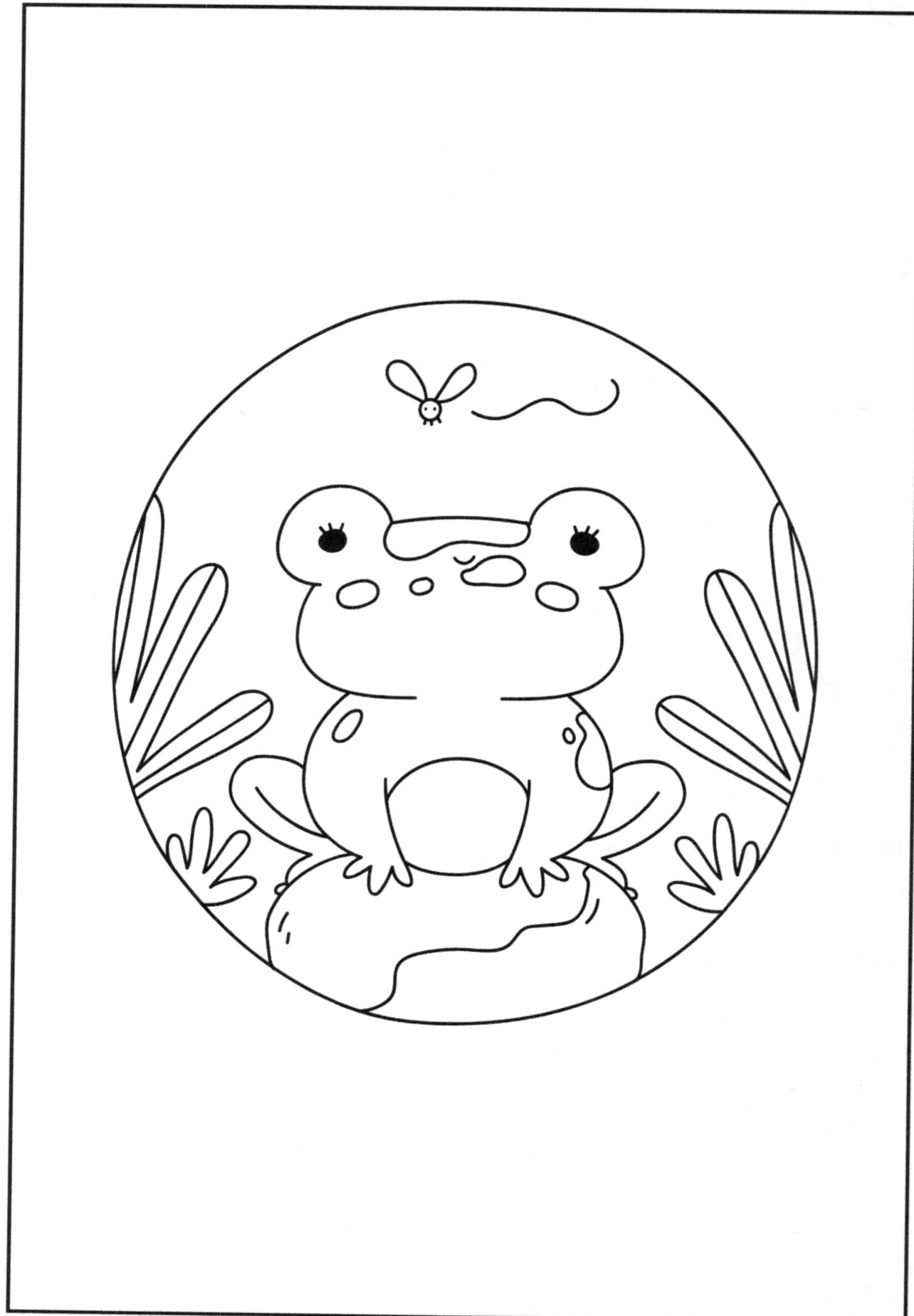